Titles b

Jude Fokwang
Mediating Legitimacy: Chieftaincy and Democratisation in
Two African Chiefdoms

Michael A. Yanou
Dispossession and Access to Land in South Africa:
an African Perspevctive

Tikum Mbah Azonga
Cup Man and Other Stories
The Wooden Bicycle and Other Stories

John Nkemngong Nkengasong
Letters to Marions (And the Coming Generations)
The Call of Blood

Amady Aly Dieng
Les étudiants africains et la littérature négro-africaine
d'expression française

Tah Asongwed
Born to Rule: Autobiography of a life President
Child of Earth

Frida Menkan Mbunda
Shadows From The Abyss

Bongasu Tanla Kishani
A Basket of Kola Nuts
Konglanjo (Spears of Love without Ill-fortune) and
Letters to Ethiopia with some Random Poems

Fo Angwafo III S.A.N of Mankon
Royalty and Politics: The Story of My Life

Basil Diki
The Lord of Anomy
Shrouded Blessings

Churchill Ewumbue-Monono
Youth and Nation-Building in Cameroon: A Study of
National Youth Day Messages and Leadership Discourse
(1949-2009)

**Emmanuel N. Chia, Joseph C. Suh & Alexandre
Ndeffo Tene**
Perspectives on Translation and Interpretation in
Cameroon

Linus T. Asong
The Crown of Thorns
No Way to Die
A Legend of the Dead: Sequel of *The Crown of Thorns*
The Akroma File
Salvation Colony: Sequel to *No Way to Die*
Chopchair
Doctor Frederick Ngenito

Vivian Sihshu Yenika
Imitation Whiteman
Press Lake Varsity Girls: The Freshman Year

Beatrice Fri Bime
Someplace, Somewhere
Mystique: A Collection of Lake Myths

Shadrach A. Ambanasom
Son of the Native Soil
The Cameroonian Novel of English Expression:
An Introduction

**Tangie Nsoh Fonchingong and Gemandze John
Bobuin**
Cameroon: The Stakes and Challenges of Governance and
Development

Tatah Mentan
Democratizing or Reconfiguring Predatory Autocracy?
Myths and Realities in Africa Today

Roselyne M. Jua & Bate Besong
To the Budding Creative Writer: A Handbook

Albert Mukong
Prisonner without a Crime: Disciplining Dissent in
Ahidjo's Cameroon

Mbuh Tennu Mbuh
In the Shadow of my Country

Bernard Nsokika Fonlon
Genuine Intellectuals: Academic and Social
Responsibilities of Universities in Africa

Lilian Lem Atanga
Gender, Discourse and Power in the Cameroonian
Parliament

Cornelius Mbifung Lambi & Emmanuel Neba Ndenecho
Ecology and Natural Resource Development
in the Western Highlands of Cameroon: Issues in Natural
Resource Managment

Gideon F. For-mukwai
Facing Adversity with Audacity

Peter W. Vakunta & Bill F. Ndi
Nul n'a le monopole du français : deux poètes du
Cameroon anglophone

Emmanuel Matateyou
Les murmures de l'harmattan

Ekpe Inyang
The Hill Barbers

JK Bannavti
Rock of God *(Kilan ke Nyiiy)*

Godfrey B. Tangwa (Rotcod Gobata)
I Spit on their Graves: Testimony Relevant to the
Democratization Struggle in Cameroon

Henrietta Mambo Nyamnjoh
"We Get Nothing from Fishishing", Fishing for Boat
Opportunies amongst Senegalese Fisher Migrants

Bill F. Ndi, Dieurat Clervoyant & Peter W. Vakunta
Les douleurs de la plume noire : du Cameroun
anglophone à Haïti

Laurence Juma
Kileleshwa: A Tale of Love, Betrayal and Corruption in
Kenya

Nol Alembong
Forest Echoes (Poems)

Marie-Hélène Mottin-Sylla & Joëlle Palmieri
Excision : les jeunes changent l'Afriaque par le TIC

Walter Gam Nkwi
Voicing the Voiceless: Contributions to Closing Gaps in
Cameroon History, 1958-2009

John Koyela Fokwang
A Dictionary of Popular Bali Names

The Earth Mother

Kehbuma Langmia

Langaa Research & Publishing CIG
Mankon, Bamenda

Publisher:
Langaa RPCIG
Langaa Research & Publishing Common Initiative Group
P.O. Box 902 Mankon
Bamenda
North West Region
Cameroon
Langaagrp@gmail.com
www.langaa-rpcig.net

Distributed outside N. America by African Books
Collective
orders@africanbookscollective.com
www.africanbookscollective.com

Distributed in N. America by Michigan State
University Press
msupress@msu.edu
www.msupress.msu.edu

ISBN: 9956-616-48-6

Contents

Synopsis

Kamsi, the Earth Mother visits the village of Nyong in the North West Region of Cameroon. She is 73 year old and has journeyed from afar. Her mission to Nyong village is to cleanse the village of all evil forces and diseases that have plagued the villagers for the past decades. After meeting with the village traditional ruler, she is given a small thatched hut to live in. It is here that villagers are instructed to come and be cleansed by her. She uses a mixture of boiled barks of trees and leaves in a large pot. A bowl is being used to dish out the liquid to the natives. Before the dish of liquid is handed over to anyone, she looks into the eyes and palms of the person and through an interpreter, identifies what maybe potentially wrong with the person. Those whose ill omens are too big are washed naked before the eyes of everyone. But a group of some notables in the village are not convinced of her supernatural gifts and are determined to expose her machinations. The chaos that ensued only goes to explain the state of affairs in the village.

Foreword

Sometime in the late 1970s and early 1980s a terrible omen befell the Bali Nyonga people of the North West Province of Cameroon. It was a visit from a mysterious and strange woman. Few remember the circumstances that surrounded the visit of the "nkamsi"-a witch doctor cum fortune-teller and exorcist. Like the story of the "la-am" or blacksmith (another fable in the Bali Nyonga folktale), no one was certain of the origin of this woman. Some said she came from the sea, from faraway lands. Yet others said she simply appeared which will explain why she was called a "nkamsi". Those who were grounded in their religious beliefs like my grandma thought she was the devil incarnate and forbade any relatives of hers to go near the demon.

False prophet or not, people came from far and near to consult with this fortune teller. And she had plenty to say. Daily processions to Bah Gwanyebit's compound became a regular sight. Before long, people started camping outside this compound so as to be early enough to receive maximum therapy. Unsanitary conditions developed as the capacity of toilet facilities became too small to accommodate the ever growing number of "patients". This did not stop the madness. Sceptics were fast becoming converts as fabulous stories of the "nkamsi's" healing powers and oracle were spreading around the village and beyond like wild fire. His Royal Highness, Galega II, and his Council at Court would also fall prey to this charlatan. Villagers who could barely sustain their livelihood were tricked into turning over their hard earned cash crops like "egusi" (melon seeds) as sacrifices to the "nkamsi" for the job of cleansing the village. In retrospect, this was a sad time for the Bali people. How could a people who had once been tricked into believing that an impending Armageddon was bound for the village, and had lost a whole clan of people *a la* Egyptian exodus be conned into thinking that their village was inhabited by demons and that unless they acted fast and swift the Kingdom was coming to its end? Unlike in the above scenario, where the Batis simply vanished from Bali after tricking them to hide in their houses, this time, no one was asked to hide in the house or run to the farm and wait for the "Passover". No, the Bali Nyonga Villagers were simply brain washed and they literarily handed over the sacredness of their traditional fabric to a make-belief goddess. More than half of the population was affected, and not even HRH and his court were spared.

As we look back on this dark period in the Bali Nyonga history, we are inclined to agree with B.F Skinner in his theory of operant conditioning, *A behaviour followed by a reinforcing stimulus results in an increased probability of that behaviour occurring in the future.* (C. George Boeree, 2006). The false prophesies and oracles recited by this "nkamsi" acted like the stimulus to the "patients" as they kept coming for more abuse and beatings at the hands of this charlatan. How else could one explain how a once rationally thinking people could be conditioned to act so irrationally? But history has taught us similar examples in Nazi Germany, Jones Town, Waco, and many other incidences where human vices have superseded reasoning.

In this master-piece drama, "The Earth Mother" by Dr. K Langmia, the audience is called to relive these painful moments in the history of the Bali Nyonga villagers. In as much as the author has used fiction to depict the situation that occurred in the Bali Nyonga village, the audience must be aware that "nkamsi" is not a myth in the Bali Nyonga folk tale. We believe that "nkamsis" appear in the village to either deliver a special message of good news or to warn the village of an impending doom. And since they are believed to be god sent, they are never invited as you can hear from Gwan-Boh in Act I Scene ii of "The Earth Mother."

The confusion that ensues from the visit of this "nkamsi" can only perhaps be likened to that of the coming of the Roman Catholic religion to Bali Nyonga. Those who worshiped gods were ordered by the "nkamsi" to surrender their gods. There were public exorcisms organized at the market square daily during this particular time period echoed by Dr. Langmia in the "Earth Mother". The height of this "traditional sacrilege" would culminate in the desecration of the "Lela Stone" by the "nkamsi." The Lela Stone is considered the symbolic centre of the traditional and cultural fabric of the Bali Nyonga Kingdom. Witnesses of this time period have surmised that this single act of defiance of the gods marked the end of and the falling apart of the Bali Nyonga traditional society and the centre has never held since. Subsequent years have seen the invasion of the "Voma Cult" by strangers, the vandalizing of the Palace which is the traditional "Holy See" of the Bali Nyonga people. HIV/AIDS has ravaged the population with vengeance. Are all these a revenge by the gods for failing to safe guard the traditional serenity of a people? We will never know.

All I can say is that Dr. Langmia has captured this time period like no other playwright could have. Many of us were kids when this event took place. We can only reminisce in this beautiful drama, The Earth Mother, and hope that while the audience enjoys itself, it is called to sympathize and take a peek at the turbulence that once rocked the peaceful life of a strong traditional society.

Lillian Fomunung
University of Tennessee Chattanooga, 2010

Dramatis Personae

1. His Royal Highness   (Village head)

2. Gwan-Kefat   Special councillor of HRH

3. Queen   Wife of the HRH

4. Kamsi   Earth Mother

5. Gwan-Boh   Member of the HRH council

6. Gwan-Njenka   Member of the HRH council

7. Gwan-Buti   Member of the HRH council

8. Gwan-Tikali   Member of the HRH council

9. Gwan-Fotoh   Member of the HRH council

10. Nah Meya   Patient

11. Nahsala   Patient

Act One

Scene One

The head of Nyong village assembles members of his council about the impending arrival of Kamsi, the Earth Mother to the village.

HRH

(Members rise as HRH makes a royal entrance. They bow and clap their hands three times before sitting down.)

Members of the council, I have summoned you here because of the visit of Kamsi. She will be arriving on «Ntambutu». The day before our market-day. So I want us to discuss how we are going to accommodate her and also present her to our people.

Gwan-kefat

(Prostrating)

"Chabufon", "Nkuyam", Lion of the forest, We have heard you. We will do all in our powers to give Kamsi a befitting welcome. We will order our wives to prepare delicious food and cook "Kwacha" and "Nkang" for her on the day of her visit.

Gwan-Tikali

(Prostrating)

"Chabufon", "Nkuyam", We want to thank you specially for organizing this visit. This is going to be a blessing for this village. We have been having sleepless nights and days because of evildoers who have inflicted pain on us. Again, thank you, Your Highness and may the ancestors continue to give you strength and wisdom to rule over us.

Gwan-Njenka

(Prostrating)

"Chabufon", "Nkuyam", I follow Ba Gwan-Tikali to salute your initiative in bringing this lady to our village. News has begun circulating about her impending arrival and I look forward to meeting her and having my protective amulets. Again, more power to your elbow, Your Highness.

Gwan-Boh

Your Highness, I thought you wanted to hear our views on the preparations to welcome Kamsi. But I have not heard a single person say where this lady will stay, how we are going to feed her every day. Whose toilet or bathroom will she use? Are we going to construct new ones for her? Who will accompany her to the market? How long is she staying here? These and many more have not been answered.

Gwan-Buti

(*Prostrating*)

"Chabufon", "Nkuyam", "Mbat Ngweya", I have heard what you've said. I have also heard what Ba Gwan-Boh has just said. I don't intend to challenge your idea of inviting a stranger to our land. I also know that all members here are not telling you the truth about what they feel. You know I speak my mind openly and bear the consequences. I have reservations for this woman's visit. I hesitate to call her a Kamsi. Kamsi do not announce their visits. They suddenly appear and take people by surprise. Those of us with grey hair sitting here know what I am talking about. This one that has openly sought an invitation from you fills my mind with doubt. Again, Your Highness, if I speak out of order, please don't throw me with the bath water.

HRH

(*Clears his throat*)

Members

"Chabufon"

HRH

Members of the council, I have heard you all. I wanted you to tell me in plain terms how you think we should accommodate our august visitor. I did not ask for lengthy speeches. I did not ask you to inform me of my duties. I know my duties. She is not my Kamsi. She is our Kamsi whose four eyes have told her that evil forces have invaded our village. She is simply using her goodwill to cleanse our village free of charge. Do you all hear?

Members

"Chabufon", We hear you.

HRH

I think Gwan-Boh was right in asking you whether you all have thought about her accommodation and food. She will be here for a while. So I expected you all to tell me your individual contributions for her successful visit. So, since you have not been able to come up with concrete arrangements, I will request that you go and sit together and brainstorm about this. The next time I summon you here, it should be a meeting where you outline a step-by-step schedule for Kamsi's visit. Do you all hear?

Gwan-Buti

(Prostrating awkwardly)

"Nkuyam", Lion of the forest, Tiger among the wild, you are the elephant and we are your claws. We fill the potholes with sand dust before you ride your horse to greet the villagers. Please let us not hurry and risk bringing home a lion's tail instead of the body. You are revered by all the four neighbouring tribes. We want you to preserve that honour as those before you have done. We have for decades respected your sound judgment on complicated village problems. But you risk rubbing your reputation in the mud by insisting that we welcome this lady. A Kamsi, your honour, is never invited. They appear and disappear after accomplishing their tasks. Do I not speak the truth? *(turning to the members)*

Members

(Silent murmurs)

Gwan-Buti

Your Highness, if you can please allow us a few more days to consult the oracle...

HRH

(Angrily)

Gwan-Buti?

Gwan-Buti

"Chabufon"

HRH

Our fathers use to say that a monkey should not rub the head of its young one to the point of cracking its skull. They also added that if a finger stays long in the anus, it will rub itself with excreta. You should know when you have crossed boundaries with your speech. Do you think I am a fool to accept the visit of this renowned Kamsi? Is it the newly arrived Christian faith in our village that is blinding you of the reality we face? Are you questioning my judgment? How dare you? (*He pauses for a while. There is an uneasy silence as members bow their heads*) You all chose me to be your village leader and now you want to challenge my decision? Now, all of you go to the council room and return within twenty-four hours with concrete plan for the visit of this lady. Gwan-Buti, it is time you choose where you belong.

(*Exits*)

Scene Two

Members of the traditional council are meeting without Gwan-Buti in their usual meeting room in the palace.

Gwan-Kefat

Dear members, I am sure you are all aware of the urgency on this matter. I may want to suggest that we divide the duties according to the skills that we possess. You are all aware I have to report to His Royal Highness on the progress we've made in twenty-four hours. What do you think? Gwan-Fotoh?

Gwan-Fotoh

Yes, I agree. Before I make my own contribution, I will request that we make this meeting less acrimonious as much as possible. We will not achieve anything if we all speak at the top of our voices. I am a specialist in palm wine tapping and roof-top thatching. I opt to provide daily palm-wine to our guest and to roof her hut whenever we select one for her.

Gwan-Njenka

I don't know about my skills. I don't think I possess any skills to help a woman of that nature. Maybe, I will just send my eldest son to help in whatever way you want me to. You know age is also weighing on me.

Gwan-Tikali

Dear members, we did not come here to hear further complains. Your Highness has given us before dawn to come up with solutions, yet Gwan-Njenka is talking about not having skills to help a woman. What kind of idea is that? This is a woman with a difference. She is four-eyed as our highness has rightly said. I am of the opinion that we summon other important villagers like quarter heads, sub-chiefs, heads of women's meeting groups, builders and other important personalities to join us in making a plan for her visit.

Gwan-Boh

Dear members, you know I am surprised that none of you have questioned the action of Your Highness in rebuking Gwan-Buti. Do you all think that Gwan-Buti was drunk when he asked those questions? I don't think so because I have begun asking some of them myself. If my memory serves me right, the last Kamsi to come to our village appeared in the compound of Ba Tanu. They woke up in the morning and saw a strange looking old man sitting on a stone in their courtyard. He then unearthed all kinds of evil objects in that compound and many other compounds in that quarter. By the time many of us waited in vain in our compound to see whether he will appear there, he had disappeared. We then slept in peace knowing that there were no evil forces around us. But now we have someone who...

Gwan-Kefat

Gwan-Boh, forgive me if I have cut into your speech. But I think we do not want to go over that contentious issue. We are here to execute the orders of His Royal Highness. Let me know those who agree with the proposal of Gwan-Tikali that we invite other important dignitaries to this meeting.

Gwan-Njenka

I agree with his decision.

Gwan-Kefat

Gwan-Fotoh, what do you think?

Gwan-Fotoh

Like Gwan-Boh, I have begun to have doubts about what we are doing?

Gwan-Kefat

Hey, nobles, I am not here to argue with you. It is often said that if you stick your finger in your anus and leave it there for too long it will become a friend of the smelling shit. I am not here to waist my time on a foregone issue. Are we looking back to the past or to the future?

Gwan-Boh

Why have you stuck you finger in the anus for too long? Why did you take it there in the first place? Have you become the tortoise who won the race against the dog by tricking it with a bone on the road? Wait for your turn to become the leader of this village to impose on us. We must weed the grass before we can be able to hoe the farm and plant seeds. Don't we members? (*Members offer their approval*) You don't expect us to jump to conclusion when we have lingering doubts in our minds about the purpose of this woman's visit.

Gwan-Fotoh

Gwan-Kefat, we all know you eat and dine with His Royal Highness even when your stomach is full. We all know that. Why are you and the His Highness pushing this kolanut quickly down our throat without offering us a cup of water? Don't you think we can choke? And if we do, will you provide us herbs when we all suffer from belly-ache? My own suggestion is that we should follow the suggestion of Gwan-Tikali but with one condition that we convince Your Highness to let us bring back Gwan-Buti among us. We all know he is full of wisdom in matters like this.

Gwan-Kefat

I strongly disagree.

Gwan-Boh

You disagree with what? The accusations levied at you or that of inviting Gwan-Buti to come back here?

Gwan-Kefat

The decision to bring back Gwan-Buti.

Gwan-Fotoh

What is your reason? Are you really siding with His Highness?

Gwan-Kefat

Dear members of the traditional council, I did not come to this meeting to settle scores with anybody. If people have their individual grudges with me let them look for the

11

appropriate moment to attack me. I am only doing my job to execute the orders of HRH. I have not taken any one's wife to bed or seized any one's piece of farmland. I don't know why some of you have decided to leave out the urgent matters of now as demanded by His Royal Highness to personally attack my character. If you think by being loyal to our chosen leader, I am acting like him, so be it. I will now take my leave and wait for you to deliberate the ways you see fit to welcome or unwelcome our humble guest.

(Exits)

Gwan-Njenka
Gwan Boh you are the cause of this.
Gwan-Boh
Who? Me? Are you out of your mind?
Gwan-Tikali
Yes, you and Gwan-Fotoh.
Gwan-Fotoh
Eh, be careful Tikali.
Gwan-Tikali
Don't call me Tikali you impotent fool.
Gwan-Fotoh
You said what? Say it again if you want to call yourself a man. I said say it again? You lecher!

(A scuffle ensues between the two of them. But they are quickly separated by Gwan-Boh and Gwan-Njenka. The sound of the village drum is heard outside.)

Gwan-Njenka
That is the sound of the village drum. I am sure Gwan-Kefat and His Royal Highness have taken a decision to summon the villagers on this issue.

Enter Queen)

Gwan-Njenka

Your Highness, a woman does not come inside…

Queen

Yes, a woman does not set foot in here but do men fight in the royal palace?

Members

We are sorry, Your Highness.

Queen

Sorry about what? For desecrating the palace? A place reserved for peace and respect of the Nyong village? How do you think His Highness feels about this?

Gwan-Tikali

Did he hear about this?

Queen

Oh yes, he did. He is aware of everything that is going on here.

Gwan-Fotoh

I am sure Gwan-Kefat is the cause of all this.

Queen

Oh no. Don't bring Gwan-Kefat into all this. Was he here when you were fighting with Gwan-Tikali? He heard it himself and you can imagine his state of mind now. He sent you out to accomplish a very important task. The task of arranging for the visit of the Earth Mother to our village. Is it because this Kamsi is a woman that suddenly you have all seen your manhood in jeopardy? Let me ask you this question. Why do you take pride in disrespecting His Highness' decision?

Gwan-Tikali

"Chabufon", we do not take pride in disrespecting our leader. We have not gone against his decision. We are just looking at how best we can welcome Kamsi so that it can be free of any incident. Please do not misunderstand us. This is how men resolve tricky issues. It will be well with us, Your Highness.

Gwan-Njenka

Please convey this message to HRH that all is well. We are indeed delighted to have Kamsi in our midst and we will do everything in our powers to give her a befitting welcome. We've just had a little disagreement. That is all. No one was fighting here. We just raised our voices a bit. Please tell him all is well and we will respect the time limit he gave us to meet him sometime today with the plan of action.

Queen

Is that a promise?

Members

That is a promise.

Queen

By the way where is Gwan-Kefat?

Gwan-Fotoh

He went to the men's room, Your Highness. He will be back.

Queen

Sure?

Gwan-Njenka

Pretty sure, Your Highness. Is there something wrong with him going to the men's room? Or do you know something that we don't know? If so, please our ears are wide opened.

Queen

I am just curious because His Highness may be concern about his absence.

Gwan-Njenka

No, he is not absent. He will be back. You may stay and wait for his return if you think we are lying.

Queen

So be it. I will leave knowing that you have all agreed that all is well with the visit of Kamsi. That is what is important. Thank you all and I wish you a successful meeting.

(Exit Queen)

Gwan-Njenka

You see. You all owe me a keg of palm wine for striking this deal.

Gwan-Boh

Ask Gwan-Tikali and Gwan-Fotoh for that.

Gwan-Njenka

Yes, you are right Gwan-Boh. Let us hear from them.

(Gwan-Tikali moves over to Gwan-Fotoh and offers him an embrace.)

Gwan-Tikali

Gwan-Fotoh, We should not be behaving like little kids. We are grown ups with titles, wives and many children.

Gwan-Fotoh

I am sorry it all started Gwan-Tikali. It will not happen again.

Gwan-Njenka

Before we leave, I think we should follow the early proposal of Gwan-Tikali. What do you think?

Members

Agreed.

Gwan-Njenka

Let us go and summon all these leaders as soon as possible. I am sure in a few hours time we will be ready with a plan for HRH.

(They Exit)

Act Two

Scene One

Villagers are squatted on stage as Kamsi addresses them. The councillors are standing behind her. The villagers come out one after the other to receive blessing from Kamsi. There is a large bowl of boiled leaves and barks of trees in front of her.

Kamsi
(Addressing the first villager. He is of middle age)
What is your name?

Numvi
Numvi.

Kamsi
Let me see your palms. Open your eyes. You have made some errors in your life. You have taken foolish decisions. But they are not very damaging. Take good care of your wives and treat them well. Do you hear me?

Numvi
Yes, Kamsi.

Kamsi
(giving him a cup of liquid medicine)
Drink all of it and come back in two weeks.

Numvi
(Drinks and goes back to his seat.)

Kamsi
(Addressing the next villager. She is an old woman) Your name?

Nah Meya
Nah Meya.

Kamsi
(Looks carefully at her. Examines her palms)
You are a wicked woman. You've sold yourself to the devil. How dare you come here to see me? You have come to test my womanhood. You will not succeed. People like you should not still be alive. You hear me?

Nah Meya

Maybe you are mistaken, your holiness. My name is Na Meya. I go to church regularly. In fact, I am a church elder. Please think again?

Kamsi

I don't need to think over. I have seen everything in your eyes and through your palms. You have hidden human bones in your closet. If you want to drink my medicine, you have to bring them out here in the open. I will not give you this medicine. It is not for the likes of you.

Nah Meya

(*Crying and going down in her knees*)
Please don't do this to me. I will do whatever it takes to clear my name. But please let me just drink half a cup of your medicine and be healed. I don't have any human bones in my closet.

Kamsi

You don't have what? You want to lie to me. You want me to undress you before the eyes of everyone here?

Nah Meya

No Please. I am innocent. Honestly, I don't know what you are talking about.

Kamsi

If you think you are pure, why did you come here for my medicine?

Nah Meya

We were told by His Royal Highness that if we don't come and be cleansed by you worse things will happen to us.

Kamsi

You are a pretender. You just don't want to tell the truth about your hidden activities to the people of this village. Since you don't want to tell me the truth, I don't want to give you my medicine because it will choke you. When you comply with my demands, I will give it to you. Next?

Nah Meya

(She rolls on the floor wailing and keening. The councillors drag her off stage.)

Nahsala

My name is Ma Nahsala.

Kamsi

How old are you?

Nahsala

I don't even know how old I am. But I was sent to marriage when I was very young. My eldest daughter tells me she is sixteen years old now. So I think I can be thirty-two years old.

Kamsi

Thirty-two years old?

Nahsala

Yes thirty-two. But I am still not very sure.

Kamsi

You know why you're not sure? It is because your secret lovers have blinded your mind. They have sucked all the juices in you and left you empty chaff.

Nahsala

With all due respect. I think I am a humble wife who is faithful to her husband.

Kamsi

Liar?

Nahsala

No Kamsi, I am not a liar.

Kamsi

Don't argue with me. The fact that you are young and beautiful does not mean that you should go back and forth with me. You hear that?

Nahsala

Yes your holiness.

Kamsi

(She grudgingly deeps her hand inside the bowl and gives her a cup of medicinal drink)
Before I see the next person. All of you listen to me.

(She moves closer to them. As she talks, she moves around in a circle.)

This village has, for years, harboured evil doers who have used it to perpetuate evil deeds. There are lots of people dying prematurely in this village. It cannot continue to happen. When I came here a few days ago, I was challenged by evil forces who sought to block my entrance. They wanted me to return. They did not want me to set foot here because they have been using this place as a sanctuary for staging their operations. That is why more and more of your children are dying young. That is why more and more of your old ones are lying sick in the hospital. The truth is that most of them will not come back alive. What you people have forgotten to know is that when witches visit your village in the night and strike at the unfortunate people, you take them directly to the government hospitals instead of seeking help from the likes of us. We are specialized in digging out talismans that have been planted in your compounds. We are specialized in rooting out those friends of yours in your traditional meetings who poison your drinks without you knowing. We are specialized in stopping those evil women who come to your dreams with axes and cutlasses to kill you while you are asleep. Oh yes, we have been chosen by the ancestors to detect all these people. Whether you like it or not, these people are sitting here with you. They have come to take my medicine without making a decision to change from their old habits. They think I cannot know them. They are the same ones who go with you to the market. They are the same ones who sing

22

with you in the meeting houses. I have determined to root them out and cast them away for life so that this village can experience peace and tranquillity. That is the reason why Your Highness invited me to come. He had heard of my activities in other villages. They are still following me where ever I go. There is no space in my compound where I come from. I would have stayed there to cater to their needs but I decided to run and come here fast before darkness falls on this beloved village.

(Noise is heard off stage. The councillors scramble to protect Kamsi. They are over-powered as a man and his wife drag in their mad son onto the stage.)

Gwan-Kefat

(Hollering)
What do you want? Kamsi doesn't attend to mad people.

Man
My son is not mad. He is sick. Somebody threw a spell on him and for over three years now, he has been living under squalid conditions in the market-place. My wife and I thought that since Kamsi is the healer sent by the ancestors, she can bring back the life of our son. He is the only son that she has with me. We want him to drink the medicinal herbs of Kamsi and be healed forever. *(Goes down on his knees before Kamsi)* Please Kamsi, don't turn my son away. He was very intelligent in school. He was hard working at home before the spells got on him. Now he eats dead rats, ticks, dead frogs and cats in the refuge at the market place. Please do what you can to bring him back to us.

Kamsi
What is his name?

Man
His name from birth is Koyila. But he is popularly known by the villagers as Pongo.

23

Kamsi

(*pointing at his wife*)
Is that his true mother?

Man

(*perplexed*)
Yes. This is his mother.

Kamsi

How many brothers and sisters does he have and do they have the same illness?

Man

No his brothers and sisters from my other wives are healthy and happy.

Kamsi

So this is the only child of this your wife?

Man

Em…Em Let her speak for herself Kamsi. (*to his wife*) Tell her all you know about him.

Wife

He is not my only child.

Kamsi

Where are the other ones? And are they living healthily with you?

Wife

They are at home and living healthily. They are all his sisters. He was the only son… and…

Man

And what? Tell her the truth. She is Kamsi and is reading your mind now. She knows all the truth.

Kamsi

Tell me the truth.

Wife

I got him out of wedlock.

Man

The truth is finally out. The truth is out. Thank you, Kamsi for using your magical powers to bring out the truth from my wife. I knew all along that this woman was hiding something from me. All along I thought that it was a spell that was cast on my son. Now I am learning something new. I always said to myself that I made a mistake in getting married to a woman from Ba Njuh's compound.

Kamsi

Ba Njuh's compound?

Man

Yes. Ba Njuh's compound. You need to know about the evil that lurks in that compound. It is often said that the owl does not hoot during the day. But it does in that compound.

Kamsi

Let me examine your son Koyila for a moment. (*Goes over and open his eyes and examines his palms.*)

Kamsi

How long has he been in this state?

Man

(*to his wife*)
Answer her!!

Wife

I don't know.

Man

You see what I was saying. She doesn't know. I said three years Kamsi. But I don't really want you to help him again? What can I do with an illegitimate child? All along I thought I was fighting to get a successor since my wives have been giving me all girls. Right now I am finished!

Kamsi

No. I will help him all the same. Go ahead and undress him. He doesn't only need to drink this medicine. I need to wash him with it.

(*She undresses Koyila with the help of The Man. She then washes him with the medicine. The villagers sing to praise Kamsi as they leave the stage*)

Scene Three

(Kamsi is having a meeting with some of the loyal councillors of His Royal Highness Viz: Gwan-Kefat, and Gwan-Njenka,)

Gwan-Kefat

Your holiness, we are here with a message from His Royal Highness. It is a message of thanks and encouragement. We are all grateful with what you are doing. The news is all over the village.

Gwan-Njenka

In fact, your holiness, you can see your success by the number of people who are lining to drink your herbal medicines. We are told that people fight to be first on the line by coming by 4a.m daily. In deed, we couldn't be more thankful.

Kamsi

I am flattered by the compliments from His Royal Highness. Really, to tell you the truth, I did not imagine the magnitude of the problem I was going to face when I agreed to his invitation. From what I have seen so far, you guys are really in deep trouble.

Gwan-Kefat

Is it really that bad?

Gwan-Njenka

Are you saying you maybe here longer that you anticipated?

Kamsi

I really don't know. I can't give you a definitive answer because each day I encounter new problems. I see that more and more of your people are living in falsehood. They carry talismans, amulets and rings on their fingers and necks that are meant to do harm. Some of them have buried charms and false gods in their enemy's compounds.

Gwan-Kefat

This is shocking.

Kamsi

That is not all. Has it dawned on you people here in this village that a lot of women are becoming more and more barren? Do you know the cause of that?

Gwan-Njenka

No. In fact we need answers. My third wife who is still very young has given birth just to one child and she is unable to bare more children. And you know what is even more annoying? That only child is a girl.

Kamsi

(with doubt)

A girl?

Gwan-Njenka

Yes a girl. What am I going to do with all the girls in my compound? I married her as my third and last wife because I was in dire need of a boy who will be my successor.

Kamsi

So you really need a boy?

Gwan-Njenka

Oh yes, I do. Can I send my third wife to come see you?

Kamsi

Oh yes, but she will have to come early like the others and take a number. I cannot make any predictions now until I examine her. Anyway, let's get back to our concerns.

Gwan-Kefat

Yes, Your holiness, maybe the way to tackle this evil in our village is to let everyone including pregnant women drink your herbal medicine. This way you wash everyone clean.

Kamsi

Not only that, I will declare a day of cleansing. This day everybody will come out to the traditional courtyard with all their gods and talismans. We will burn all of them.

Gwan-Njenka

Burn all of them?

Kamsi

Yes, Burn all of them. I have already seen that for me to do
a thorough cleansing, your village needs a face lift.

Gwan-Njenka

I have the gods and talisman left for me by my late father.
They have protected me and my family for all these years. I
throw libations on them every evening before I go to sleep.
Are you saying that you will burn all that?

Gwan-Kefat

I don't think this is what she is referring to.

Gwan-Njenka

What are you referring to?

Kamsi

I am going to see the ones that are good and allow them to
be taken home. But I need to see all of them before I make
the decision. I am sure His Highness brought me here to do
my job well.

Gwan-Kefat

Of course, no one is beating the drum of failure for your
initiative. We have a saying that if you don't spend
considerable time with the sick, you will never know what
it means to be sick. I think, you are right to see all what we
have so as to winnow the grain from the chaff.

Kamsi

Definitely. And that is why I said I may need additional
time to accomplish my task. I'm sure His Highness
understands the urgency with which this work entails. You
need to convey that to him.

Gwan-Njenka

I think he knows.

Kamsi

If I don't cleanse your village, you may soon witness an
extinction of an entire generation.

Gwan-Kefat

(shocked)

An entire generation? Are you just joking or…

29

Kamsi

I mean it.

Gwan-Njenka

So how long can you achieve this?

Kamsi

I really don't know. All I need is patience and loyalty. If I get cooperation from you people, I will do this in five months. But if I keep getting the kinds of people who have appeared before me all the time, then, I may have to need additional help.

Gwan-Kefat

You know part of our duty was to come and get first hand information from you on what you need to carry out your job effectively. His Royal Highness needs to be informed about your needs so he can do all in his powers to help.

Gwan-Njenka

So can you be more specific on the things you need. What kinds of additional help were you referring to? Do you need us to bring our own witchdoctors and diviners to work with you or by additional help you mean people outside our village?

Kamsi

What did you say? Did I hear you mention witchdoctors and diviners?

Gwan-Njenka

Oh yes. We have powerful Seers in the village who can lend a helping hand if need be.

Kamsi

So where were they before your village was thrown into chaos? Where were they when evil forces were planting dangerous seeds on almost all your road paths?

Gwan-Kefat

I think the problem is that most of them have become old and tired over the years.

Gwan-Njenka

And they've not been properly rewarded. Maybe that is the reason behind their lack of interest. But I can say for the past hundred or so years, they've been quite good at protecting our land from bad people.

Kamsi

Do you know what? I will burn them alive.

Gwan-Njenka/Gwan-Kefat

(Taken aback)

Burn them alive?

Kamsi

Oh yes, burn them and expose them to the eyes of everyone.

Gwan-Kefat

Please your holiness, can you be more compassionate? How can you say that of men you really don't know?

Gwan-Njenka

I am sure you meant some of them. Not many though. Most of them have helped in curing the sick and the blind. I am sure Your Highness will not be pleased to hear that from you.

Kamsi

Really? You are quite sure he will not be pleased? Do you know that was my primary mission here? Do you know why they have so far not had the courage to step foot on my compound? Look, what I see, your naked eyes cannot see. What I hear, your human ears cannot hear. I talk and dine with the unseen forces and they are the winds that are taking me to wherever and I have no other reason but to obey the forces of the wind. I cannot ignore their whispers and turn a blind eye on a target that they have instructed me to get rid of. So what I am telling you about your so-called diviners and seers is that they are self-imposed and self-appointed. They have deceived you for years and that is why suffering goes on endlessly in this village.

Gwan-Kefat

(Supplicating)

Your holiness, consider our queries as having been uttered in ignorance. We are humans as you rightly said and what you super human beings can see, if given thousand eyes, we cannot see.

Gwan-Njenka

Forgive us. We were just echoing our thoughts. We did not know that we had to think our words carefully before uttering them. Please when you meet with HRH, let him not know about this otherwise we risk losing our titles and positions in the palace. We have worked too hard to earn the positions we currently occupy.

Kamsi

Did you all come here to tempt me?

Gwan-Njenka/Kefat

(Supplicating on their knees)

We beg you to pity us. We are just messengers of His Royal Highness.

Kamsi

Did His Highness tell you to come and test my supernatural powers?

All

No he did not.

Kamsi

Then why have you all decided to play the devil's advocate?

All

We are sorry. Please have pity. Please don't be angry.

Kamsi

Are you sorry for betraying your leader or you are sorry for making me angry?

All

Both, your holiness.

Kamsi

Then I will have to meet His Royal Highness after this and tell him of my decision to leave this village as soon as possible.

Gwan-Kefat

Please don't. In the name of God in Heaven, please don't do this. It will be an abomination of the first order.

Gwan-Njenka

We will not only lose our positions and titles but we will be exiled from this village. And what will happen to our wives and children. I dread to think about it.

Gwan-Kefat

Please what kind of amends do you want from us. We are ready to satisfy you just to save this village.

Gwan-Njenka

Yes tell us. We will pay. I have goats, cows and pigs.

Gwan-Kefat

I have land and people who can accompany you to work for free.

Gwan-Njenka

Honestly, you are right. We must burn all the talismans and charms in this village. I will go and burn mine right away.

Gwan-Kefat

Me too. Please go ahead and expose all the diviners and false priests calling themselves diviners in this village. I will even go as far as providing you with some names.

Kamsi

(Pauses)

Now I know all your secrets. Now leave before I use my magic powers to cripple you before you reach your destinations.

Act Three

Scene One

(GwanTikali, Gwan Boh, Gwan-Fotoh and Gwan Buti are meeting in Gwan-Buti's compound).

Gwan-Buti
Gentlemen, now that the cattle have grazed up to the hut, we need to build fences. We brought this to ourselves, so there is no escape.

Gwan-Fotoh
Gwan-Buti, you can't blame this on us. You know who to blame. You and I saw this coming.

Gwan-Tikali
Are we here to cast blames or to look for solutions?

Gwan-Boh
We are here for both. Our fathers used to say that before you go out searching for sick leaves, you must know what caused the ailment. We need to know so as to avoid making more mistakes in future.

Gwan-Fotoh
I know Gwan-Buti is blaming most of us for dancing to the tune of His Royal Highness in the first place. We were cowards. He was the only lone lion in our midst to fight with the elephant.

Gwan-Tikali
Gwan-Buti, we honour your service. We respect your foresight. We blame ourselves for failing to see the havoc this woman was going to cause. Now tell us what steps we should take to restore pride and peace in the land. Our people have been hurt. They are angry. They want urgent action.

Gwan-Boh
Gwan-Tikali, you have echoed my thoughts.

Gwan-Fotoh
I agree. Let's hear from Gwan-Buti.

Gwan-Buti

I want you all to go to Gwan-Kefat and tell him to inform his master that Kamsi is no longer wanted by the people. If he refuses to heed, march straight to the palace.

Gwan-Fotoh

You won't come along?

Gwan-Tikali

No. He doesn't need to.

Gwan-Fotoh

Why?

Gwan-Boh

Why? What kind of dumb question is that?

Gwan-Fotoh

Is that meant to be an insult?

Gwan-Boh

Definitely. How can someone like you with gray hair and all sorts of titles bestowed upon you not be aware of the role of Gwan-Buti in a crisis of this nature. I mean, it is a shame to our tradition to have someone of your calibre to sit in the council of elders when indeed you carry ignorance on your face.

Gwan-Fotoh

Enough. I say enough of this. Is it because I won the land dispute with you, or it is because I caught you in the farm making it with Gwan-Buti's youngest wife that you have the effrontery to say this to me? I say enough of this else I expose all…

(Gwan Boh leaps from his seat and dashes at Gwan-Fotoh. They roll on the floor in a fight that is quickly separated by the elders?)

Gwan-Buti

Ehm Ehm…

Gwan- Boh

(Sprawling on the feet of Gwan-Buti)

Forgive me Gwan-Buti. I did not mean to hurt you.

Gwan-Buti
Have I said anything to you?

Gwan-Boh
No. But the palm wine tapper needs not hear the sound of his calabash to know that it is broken. He can read the cracks on it.

Gwan-Tikali
"Mfedba", the grains have already spilled from the bag. Let us not mix it with sand. We came here for one purpose. To seek help from our most revered elder Gwan-Buti to resolve the village crisis caused by Kamsi. It was not about Fotoh and Gwan-Boh. Theirs can wait. That of Kamsi cannot. (*Turning to Gwan-Buti*). Gwan-Buti, do I speak in one accord with you?

Gwan-Buti
(*Silently angry. Looks scornfully at Gwan-Boh and then slowly leaves the stage*)

Gwan-Tikali
(*Shaking his head*)
The goat's head has fallen on its back. Thunder will soon clatter. Gwan-Fotoh and Gwan-Boh, you all get ready for the inevitable.

Gwan-Fotoh
Gwan Boh or me? Please address your comment to the one who warmed himself comfortably on the hairy cushion of someone else's she-goat.

Gwan-Tikali
Enough of this nonsense! Stop the insults! (*Subdued*) Now in order to solve the larger problem that confronts us, we must confront the tiny ones. So I suggest we go in and meet Gwan-Buti. Gwan-Boh, I am afraid you may have to go home to your family. We will inform you later on the result of our mission.

(*They exit*)

Scene Two

(His Royal Highness is having a meeting with Kamsi, The Queen and Gwan-Kefat)

HRH

Kamsi, I have invited you to know about your activities so far. Can you tell us how you've been going about your work?

Kamsi

Your Highness, I feel honoured to have been invited by you to discuss how my work has been done so far. Again, let me take this opportunity to thank you, your councillors and particularly the villagers for welcoming me with open arms in this village. The beautiful compound and the hut built for me have seen steady flow of visitors with food, drinks and gifts of appreciation for what I have done in changing their lives. Your Highness, with your permission, let me tell you of this particular incident that actually sums up my entire two weeks campaign to root out evil doers in this village. There is this case of Nah Meya who came to drink my medicine but I refused to give it to her because of what I saw through her palms and eyes. I am sure Gwan-Kefat knows this particular incident.

HRH

Is that true Gwan-Kefat?

Gwan-Kefat

Yes it is true Your Highness. I know about this lady in question.

HRH

Go ahead Kamsi

Kamsi

Your Highness, I saw evil in this woman. I said before the hearing of everyone present that "You have hidden human bones in your closet. If you want to drink my medicine, you have to bring it out here in the open. I will not give you this medicine." I bet you, she swore before me that I have mistaken her for someone else. She said, she is a church woman, and she even belongs to the council of church elders. But I looked again and my guts told to me to decline the offer. But when everyone had gone, this very woman returned to my hut at midnight when I was asleep and woke me up with a loud knock on my door. I opened the door to find her standing with the bones I talked about wrapped in a nylon paper. She said she had come to ask for repentance. She then asked me if she can come in the morning like the rest of the villagers to drink my medicine because I had made her the subject of ridicule in the village. So this is the kind of situation I have encountered thus far.

HRH

Gwan-Kefat, Is that what you heard?

Gwan-Kefat

Your Highness, I know about the situation where she was called evil when she came for the medicine. But that part of her coming back in the middle of the night I was not there and cannot say anything about it. But it is possible.

HRH

Does my queen know anything about this story?

Queen

Your Highness, The story of Nah Meya has gone beyond this village. Everyone is talking about it.

HRH

What are they saying? What have you heard from your own sources about her and the activities of Kamsi?

Queen

Your highness, I can only speak about what I have heard from women. Maybe Gwan-Kefat can tell you more from men's point of view. Again, this is just from the reports that some women have said to me in private or to the other queens. They have applauded the work of Kamsi. They say she is patient and gifted with extra-ordinary strengths to attend to thousands of villagers in just two weeks alone. They think that indeed, she is the real Kamsi.

HRH

What about the men, Gwan-Kefat?

Gwan-Kefat

Your Highness, I think they have also reacted the same way as the queen has mentioned. I don't have anything different to say. (*Turning to Kamsi*) You are a great healer, Kamsi. You have been doing a spectacular job. We thank you for all that you've done so far for us.

Kamsi

Thank you too. And if I may add something Your Highness, I think from what you've heard from them and from many others, I have to first of all be grateful to you. You took the risk and pain to invite me here. I did not know the enormity of work that was waiting for me. It has been exciting and at the same time challenging.

HRH

We are indeed grateful to you too Kamsi. By challenge, do you mean difficulties that need our help?

Kamsi

Some of it Your Highness. Some of the challenges I have been facing is to work hand in hand with the women. If the queen can help me to sensitize them to be more cooperative, I will be delighted.

Queen

I will do anything you want to make you comfortable.

HRH

So your problem is with women, not men?

Kamsi

(*Throws a quick glance at Gwan-Kefat*)
Yes, Your Highness.

(A *sound of someone clearing his throat is heard outside. It is Gwan-Njenka.* Enter Gwan-Njenka)

Gwan-Njenka

Your Highness, I am not intruding. I went to visit my old friend Gwan-Kefat but was told by his young daughter that he was here in the palace. I came running thinking the village was on fire because he never comes to the palace without passing through my home. I am very sorry for the interruption. Since I have seen all of you in peace, I can now take my leave.

HRH

Wait a minute. I don't think you did wrong to come and look for your friend. Our fathers used to say being alone is as worse as contracting a disease. By coming here, you have shown that both of you have a common bond. I thank you for checking on your friend. I will not want you to leave. In fact, he did not inform you of his coming because I summoned him to come in a hurry not because the village was on fire but because I wanted him to be a witness to the brief recount of Kamsi's activities ever since she has been with us.

Gwan-Njenka

"Chabufon" "Nguyam" Lion of the forest. Your words are as sweet as a fresh palm wine in the morning. Your words have soothed my pounding heart. Your Royal Highness, champion of all warriors and valiant ruler of this proud village, I came running like a he-goat on heat with my sword and dagger thinking that enemies have captured us in broad day light. Let me seize this opportunity to implore you and praise you for bringing Kamsi to us. She has been a great blessing to the village.

HRH

So what do the people say so far about her healing powers?

Gwan-Njenka

I have not heard anything suspicious.

HRH

You mean you've not heard any positive or negative words about what she has been doing?

Gwan-Njenka

(Glances at Gwan-Kefat and gets an affirmative look).
No. Nothing. I think everything has been great.

Kamsi

Your Highness, Maybe Gwan-Njenka has heard something negative. I don't mind listening to it. It only helps me improve for the better.

Gwan-Njenka

I don't have any. My wives and children have drunk your medicine and they seem contended. Maybe others have heard other things but I Gwan-Njenka from Njenka quarter is still to hear anything negative about our great Kamsi.

HRH

Well Kamsi, thank you for the wonderful job you've been doing so far. I summoned this initial meeting to learn firsthand how you've been doing. I like things being said in the open. Since they have confirmed that all is well, who am I to guess that there is something wrong out there. You have heard from my wife, the queen, Gwan-Kefat and now Gwan-Njenka. I want to let you know that because you are doing this marvellous job, your stay will be extended and your reward will double . *(To the Queen)* Please take Kamsi to the refreshing room and give her whatever you women have prepared for her to thank her for all her services to the village.

(Exit Queen and Kamsi)

Now Councillors, tell me about the attitudes of Gwan-Buti, Gwan-Boh, Gwan-Fotoh and Gwan-Tikali. Have they been cooperative?

Gwan-Kefat

Your Highness, now that the hawk has hovered into the sky, the chickens can roost. The truth is that we are in a big mess. Gwan-Buti and the other traitors have rallied the villagers for an uprising if you don't send Kamsi away.

HRH

Why?

Gwan-Njenka

(*Peeping away to see if Kamsi can hear him*)
Your Highness, it all started at the preparatory meeting you told us to have. Gwan-Buti and the others decided to create havoc for this woman even before she arrived.

HRH

Let me know the havoc they've created. I think I will order their excommunication from the village tonight.

Gwan-Kefat

Not so fast Your Highness. It may explode the situation. I think you should strip them of all the councillor privileges. They think more and more resources have been wasted on an ignorant woman. I have even overheard Gwan-Buti plotting your downfall because of this.

HRH

(*Furiously*)
Me!!!! You mean me! Or someone else?

Gwan-Njenka

All of them. Gwan-Boh, Gwan-Tikali and Gwan-Fotoh. They want to use this dissatisfaction with Kamsi to get at you. I suspect that one of your wives may have something to do with Gwan-Boh. But I am not sure. I saw him talking to one of them at the market.

Gwan-Kefat

I don't think they were only talking. My first wife has actually confirmed to me that they have been making it in the farm.

HRH

Why am I learning about all these now?

Gwan-Kefat

Your Highness, it is said that if you hear noise from the chicken-hut at night know that it has been visited by a python. You wanted to know about Gwan-Buti and his allies. If you did not inquire we couldn't have known what you want to hear and what you don't want to hear.

Gwan-Njenka

And if you are still interested, You Highness, these traitors have gone as far as recruiting trouble-makers to disrupt the big bamboo stick ceremony of Kamsi coming up in a few days.

HRH

What? The big what?

Gwan-Kefat

Kamsi has summoned the entire village to come out on a certain day on the big « Lela» platform to witness her miracle of cleansing the village. Men are expected to come out with extremely long Indian bamboo sticks with five holes on them and women with walking sticks rubbed with camwood.

HRH

But what is wrong with that?

Gwan-Njenka

There is nothing wrong about the stick. But Gwan-Buti and his allies see this as exploitation of the people.

HRH

What has bringing sticks from the bush to do with exploitation of the people? Is there something you people are not telling me?

Gwan-Njenka

I think at this juncture we have to be very open to you. It seems as if Kamsi is sometimes rude to the villagers. You know I couldn't say that in her presence.

Gwan-Kefat

Your Highness, Gwan-Buti and his followers still think that she is not the right Kamsi.

HRH

Why do you think they still think that way? Was it bad for me to bring this woman here? You were here when we had the visit from her emissary?

Gwan-Njenka

They still think that way because in the past Kamsi's just appeared. They were never known. I think your late father used to meet a couple of them only after they had silently performed their deeds in the darkest hour of night usually with no one present. But she has a completely different approach.

HRH

All right. What do you propose we do with all these burning issues?

Gwan-Kefat

I think if we get rid of these traitors the village will be at peace.

Gwan-Njenka

I think so too.

HRH

What do you mean get rid of them? You mean the excommunication I talked about?

Gwan-Kefat

No I think we should rather mysteriously eliminate them.

Gwan-Njenka

You should first strip them of their titles and appoint new members to fill their positions.

HRH

Who do you have in mind to fill their positions?

(*Knock at the door. It is the queen*)

Queen

Your Highness, I am sorry to interrupt. It is Kamsi who wants to talk with you privately before she leaves.

HRH

Tell her to meet me in the other chamber. I will be there in a short while. (*She exits*) Gentlemen, Go home and think about strategies we can use to achieve all our objectives in the face of all these challenges. Thank you for all your advice.

(*They exit*)

Scene Three

(In front of the royal palace courtyard. All the villagers are assembled. Men with long «Indian bamboo» sticks and women with walking sticks rubbed with camwood. All the councillors are present)

Kamsi

I want to thank you all for obeying my orders. Today we are going to finally cleanse the evil that has affected this village for decades. I will be telling you what to do with what you have. First of all, I want the women to be on my left while the men move to my right.

(They move gradually)

Gwan-Kefat

(Whispering to Kamsi)

I just want you to know that Gwan-Buti and his entourage are around and fully armed.

Kamsi

Listen everyone. I have been reliably informed that some people have come here purposely to create disorder. I want to assure those men who think they are real men to try anything dirty to disrupt this occasion. They will pay for it with their entire family. If you think I am wasting my time and effort to do a job for which I am not being paid sufficiently, go ahead with your devilish plans. We will see whether it is you who is the Kamsi or I who has all the powers from above.

Villagers

(They murmur)

Kamsi

Listen everyone. I will give orders on how we are going to conduct this event. I will start with the women. Raise your walking sticks. I will go around and perform my usual ritual.

(*She moves around and selects a few women to come up front*) These four women standing in front of me are unclean. I will ask them to place their sticks on the floor. We will burn them.

Gwan-Buti

(*Stepping forward*)
Why will you burn their sticks?

Gwan-Kefat

It is not your place to interfere with the activities of the gods.

Gwan-Njenka

Yes, You have no right to ask Kamsi any questions whatsoever. She has been authorized by His Royal Highness. I think your questions have been misdirected.

Gwan-Buti

I want to know why my wife is among the four selected. Was it a plan?

Gwan-Fotoh

But why are both of you acting on her behalf. Let her defend herself.

Kamsi

Defend myself against what or whom? Who are these people? I have never seen both of you. You have never exposed your evil machinations to me until now. And you ask me to defend myself. What am I defending myself for? Why will someone who calls himself a councillor to His Royal Highness ask me why I want to burn the sticks of four women whose sticks have been infected? Why will he ask me why his wife is among the four selected? Is he suspecting foul play?

Gwan-Buti

Yes I am suspecting foul play.

Gwan-Kefat

Please stop this childish interruption, Gwan-Buti.

Gwan-Buti

Gwan-Kefat? Or whatever you call yourself. Why are you so interested in me and my interruptions? Do you have something to hide? Have you had nocturnal meetings with Kamsi and His Royal Highness about me and my entourage? What have you people said about us? Do you want me and my group to expose you and His Royal Highness? I don't think so. If you are wise enough let this great guest answer simple questions.

Gwan-Tikali

Gentlemen, If I can say something, I will greatly appreciate it. Kamsi? We are here with long sticks for what we do not know. You have been here getting to three weeks and all we hear from our wives and children and visitors to your shrine are horrible stories. We have come here just because our Highness supports your initiative and we never disobey our leader. But we have concerns.

Gwan-Boh

Part of the concern we have is that you have brought us more shame than honour. If you think I am making it up, point to one success story. Is it the issue with Nah Meya or that with Koyila alias Pongo. Nah Meya has been sleepless ever since and she has opened all her closets to everyone to see that she has no human bones stuck in there. She has even sworn before the tomb of her late parents. Koyila's illness has instead worsened ever since she drank your medicine. Many more villagers are complaining of stomach ache. So tell us why it is so?

Gwan-Kefat

She has not ordered us here to answer questions. She performs rituals.

(Exits angrily)

Gwan-Njenka

As I earlier said, she has orders to do what is right for our village.

Gwan-Buti

Why are you not leaving like your brother in kind. Isn't it said that two cocks searching for a prey never move in opposite direction? So you want to defend her alone?

Gwan-Njenka

Gwan-Buti. I want to let you know about the consequences of your action. You are flexing your muscle with His Royal Highness and you are using this poor woman to achieve your objectives. You will see.

(Exits angrily)

Gwan-Buti

(Addresses the entire villagers)
Kwa kwa ye!!!

Villagers

Ye!

Gwan-Buti

"Wo wo liba liba?"

Villagers

Ha yah wo wo ha yah.

Gwan-Buti

Musigong ni nju ni tsu mi?

Villagers

Ha yah wo wo ha yah.

Gwan-Buti

Mun ni wu wuni yi?

Villagers

Ha yah wo wo ha yah.

Gwan-Buti

Men do not run from a fight. They confront it with courage. We know where Gwan-Kefat and Gwan-Njenka have disappeared to? They have gone to inform His Royal Highness that we have come to disrupt the activities of Kamsi. That is not our objective. We only want Kamsi to answer our questions. She is still with us. We want to assure you that we will not kidnap you. We only want answers. (*Addressing the villagers*) A few weeks ago before Kamsi came to this village, we had a meeting in the palace with His Royal Highness. I heard all what the councillors said and I was not pleased. I said and will say it here before you all. If I am telling a lie let the ghost of my forefathers strike me dead. I told His Royal Highness that Earth Mothers that we grew up knowing were never invited. They appeared and disappeared. If they are invited, then something fishy must be going on. Maybe HRH has a special motive for inviting her. Maybe she bought her way. No one knows at this juncture. But all I want to say is that we have spent enough time, money and energy for her with no good results.

Villagers

(*Gestures of approval*)

Gwan-Buti

That is what I said. I gave examples upon examples on Kamses that came to this village when I was still a child. I remember only knowing about them after their deeds had been done. They were never invited. They never slept in the village. They never invited people's wives and children to disgrace them in public. Now we have this Kamsi who is making families split and children disappear for fear of her wrath. She has not shown us any proof of all the cases she is saying have been uncovered. (*To Kamsi*) Show us the evidence.

Villagers

Show us the evidence!!!!

(*Enter village Juju, «Mubuh» accompanied by Gwan-Kefat and Gwan-Njenka, All the villagers go on their knees except the councillors*)

Kamsi

(Being led by Gwan-Kefat and Gwan-Njenka)
Please let me out of here. They have insulted and assaulted me in broad day light. I need to speak to His Royal Highness.

Gwan-Kefat

Gwan-Buti. You looked for it. You are going to get it. It is man that is afraid of darkness not the owl. When a dog eats a frog, its next resting place is the grave. You want to fight His Royal Highness without measuring the length and sharpness of your sword.

Gwan-Njenka

It is now time for invisible powers to fight among themselves. No more empty talk. Only the sound of gun powder at a grave side will be heard. Well, all of you standing and supporting Gwan-Buti should not say I and Gwan-Kefat never warned you. You have used your own finger and touched your anus with it. Now go and sleep in ever lasting peace.

Gwan-Buti

(Laughing)
Kwa Kwa ye?

Villagers

Ye

Gwan-Kefat

Wo ho liba liba?

Villagers

Ha yah wowo ha yah

Gwan-Buti

Musigong ni nju ni tsu mi?

Villagers

Ha yah wowo ha yah

Gwan-Buti

Mun ni wu wu ni yi?

Villagers

Ha yah wow o ha yah.

Gwan-Buti

Nothing will happen. Darkness will follow the path of evil.

Gwan-Boh

The river will continue to flow downwards.

Gwan-Tikali

And the moon will continue to shine in the dark.

Gwan-Buti

Our goats will only eat grass while our pigs will only feed on coco-yams. Not the reverse!

(Some women are heard crying)

Gwan-Kefat

The oil lamps will soon be depleted of kerosene.

Gwan-Fotoh

And darkness will fall.

(Clatters of bamboo sticks are heard and the loud cries of women wailing are rising as the councillors are fighting among themselves. «Mubuh» stealthily exits with Kamsi)